TARA TYSON

Two Birds And A Lot More Stones

Copyright © 2024 by Tara Tyson

All rights reserved. No part of this publication may be reproduced, stored or transmitted in any form or by any means, electronic, mechanical, photocopying, recording, scanning, or otherwise without written permission from the publisher. It is illegal to copy this book, post it to a website, or distribute it by any other means without permission.

First edition

*This book was professionally typeset on Reedsy.
Find out more at reedsy.com*

Contents

Devastation of the heart	1
Ready to run	3
Masterpiece	4
The Speaker Says	5
Wishing I Could Believe	6
Honesty	7
Both Mine and Yours	8
Oblivion	9
The Leopard	10
Senseless Injustice	11
Laid Ahead	12
Phoenix	13
Too Much, You Whore	14
Jungle Creatures	15
Green Gloomy Grass	16
Icarus	17
STAGGERING	18
Source of Pain	19
Blurred Boundaries	20
And	21
3 Lines, 3 Words	22
Unbroken Spell	23
Speaking Bodies	24
Questionable	25
Get Back	26

Pain? Beauty?	27
Resurrection	28
Dwelling	29
Caged	30
Time and Time	31
Breaking Down	32
Outcast	33
Imperfectly Perfect	34
I am…	35
A Past Love	36
My Body?	37
Sacred Scars	38
Fish	39
Basket	40
Salt Tears	41
Lurking Bitterly	42
Cigarettes	43
Weather Forecast	44
Tried and Failure Shelf	45
Imaginary Monsters	46
For Georgina	47
Hunched is the Rook	48
Unconditional	49
Ramblings of Anger	50
Petition	52
What Makes A Monster	53
Rotten Pears	54
Free?	56
Stress	57
Suicide is a Sin, They Say.	59
Drained of Colour	61

Leave	62
Riding Once Again	63
Firefly Stars	64
I Wish You Happiness	65

Devastation of the heart

Pt.1

But the heart brings devastation that the mind creates for us
And when we say no, the heart beats us down
And logic says stop, but we cannot,
Ironically,
If we stop our self-destruction,
We meet two birds, one pity, one sorrow.
Soon to become our only friends, these birds.
The beginning, the middle and the end.
And the sun might rise again if we ask it to nicely;
But it's just the devastation of the heart.

Pt.2

And when we say no, the heart beats us down.
The beginning, the middle and the end.
But this is just the devastation of the heart.
And logic says stop, but we cannot,
Though we stop our self-destruction,
But the heart brings devastation that the mind creates for us,
And we meet two birds, one pity, one sorrow,

TWO BIRDS AND A LOT MORE STONES

Soon to become our only friends, these birds;
Ironically.
But the sun might rise again if we ask it to nicely.

Ready to run

I feel something is near;
I think it's getting closer.
I know it is there;
I am ready to run.

I pretend not to notice it.
I worry that it knows I know;
I try and disguise my fear.
I am ready to run.

I imagine it goes away.
I smile ironically;
I know it won't.
I hope I am ready to run.

Masterpiece

Between my finger and thumb, I balance the thought of life.

If dying is an art,
Let me be the masterpiece.

The Speaker Says

The speaker says please stop
The listener hears please stop noticing me
The witness notices her.

The speaker says fuck off
The listener hears the same words but won't
The witness notices how much she needs him.

The speaker says I need help
The listener hears I'm fine
The witness notices a struggling, helpless shell of a person.

The speaker says hello
The listener hears goodbye
The witness watches her fade away.

Wishing I Could Believe

I feel slightly wobbly;
I think like I might tilt over.
I know some might admire me;
I am beautiful some may say.

I pretend I believe these lies.
I worry that if I fall I won't get up;
I try to stay stable, no relapse please.
I am struggling.

I imagine a world where I am perfect;
I smile hoping it will show truly.
I hope I can admire myself like they admire me.
I am wishing I could believe.

Honesty

It was honesty they craved,
The black and white simplicity
It happens when no one spoke but stared,
It sounds like hum and buzz of silence
But no one would speak and there was no honesty at all.

Both Mine and Yours

Tears gathered at your ankles,
A puddle of tears and blood,
Do you stop or carry on, can you do either?
So you do nothing and nothing changes.

A puddle of tears and blood
Both mine and yours
So you do nothing and nothing changes
A puddle of our tears and our blood.

Both mine and yours
We are together, as one
A puddle of our tears and our blood
We comfort each other.

We are together, as one
Do you stop or carry on, can you do either?
We comfort each other
Tears gathered at your ankles.

Oblivion

Only the children still laughed
Oblivious to the adults' silence
For they were the ones who knew the truth
The truth of laughter is depression hiding in the children's chatter.

Oblivious to the adults' silence
We sat and stared into the abscess of darkness
The truth of laughter is depression hiding in the children's chatter It dwelt in the hearts of the most innocent.

We sat and stared into the abscess of darkness
No light, no hope
It dwelt in the hearts of the most innocent
The abscess of light or was it darkness?

No light, no hope
For they were the ones who knew the truth
The abscess of light or was it darkness
Only the children still laughed.

The Leopard

Soft, padding paws
Soft, silky fur
You lay down by my feet
A twitch of the tail
A black spot at its end
And you settle calmly, peacefully next to me.

Senseless Injustice

This mighty city shows senseless injustice, incomprehensible, absent minded humans,
In their wretched condition life turns against one,
They no longer had any appetite for life
But yet in their total despair
Through their hostile existence were two birds.
One white, one black.
The white one had an aimless gaze that seemed unable to settle upon one in particular.
The black one was living flames, trying to tempt me from this wearisome drab place.
Do I follow or remain with the white one whose wings glistened with an unreal sparkle.
Fake happiness yet happiness it was,
Or do I follow the black one who offered to show me the truth,
Deep and dark no doubt but surely not knowing is far worse.

Laid Ahead

Little did they know the danger that laid ahead
Give me protection precious horse; save me from what lies ahead
Don't think about the darkness and the depression
They say the horses and the tribes will protect you but they still had doubts
Which grew stronger as they rode down the mountain, into the danger that laid ahead.

Phoenix

O Ella we'll burn that bridge when we get to it
The flames will keep us warm
The destruction will fuel us
Into building a better future or destroying the present day.

Has anyone heard
Of a phoenix; that rises from the ashes
And lives again but
Does it live a better life after death than the life we struggle with now.

Too Much, You Whore

Too much on show, you whore
Too little, you prude
Where's the balance between slut and cool
How much skin does society make you show
Just to feel part of that crowd
They question you when you cover your scars
But judge you when you leave them on show.
How do people fit in to this clique part of the world
Where only your skin defines you,
Tell me is it true that pain is beauty?

Jungle Creatures

The jungle of your mind,
Only you can decipher its ropes and branches
Only you can hear the cry of crickets and the growls of panthers
Only you can go to the vet depths, the deepest darkest part of the jungle.
Can you see in the darkness amiss the ferns and bracken?
Can you follow the light out to the safety of the meadow?
Or are you stuck, trapped, wrapped in vines head to toe, Being strangled by the python that slips round your neck, Being bitten by mosquitoes thirsting for your blood?
Are you king of the jungle, it's mighty ruler, or are you a victim of its harsh governing
Forever in shadow, forever in dark, barely able to put one foot in front of the other
Too tired, too drained, too exhausted to continue fighting those vines, the python and the mosquitoes again and again.

Green Gloomy Grass

They say the grass is greener on the other side,
A place where the sun always shines
But no one ever notices or mentions
That the greenest grass needs rain to grow
And rainy days may be dark,
But the sun will shine again on the other side
And your vision of a pretty field with a beautiful rainbow appears again
But no one ever sees the gloomy days that it went through, To become this beautiful.

Icarus

The birds flew with undoubtable grace,
Such poised elegance,
As smooth as a ballerina leaping into the air,
But yet these birds could fly,
Up and up they went,
Like Icarus to the sun
But their wings did not melt and they soared in the sky with such beauty That even the senseless humans had no choice but to watch them.

STAGGERING

Slowly waking from a slumber so deep
Tired eyes blinking in the sudden light
And sore limbs you start to stretch
Get up and move you think but you can't
Get up and go, you try but it's difficult
Everyone moans about how slow you are
Rising out of bed each morning
Inside you know you have to but you hate it
Not because you're tired, but because you have to face another day, alive
Give yourself a chance to make today a better day.

Source of Pain

Finding the source of pain was difficult,
   She looked all around herself,
   The people, the things they said
   But it only enhanced her grief
   The places, the way they stared down at her,
   But it only showed her fear,
   The world around her was toxic
   Full of monstrosities and lies
   But that was not the source of pain,
   Because when she looked inside herself she found what she was looking for, The source of pain.

Blurred Boundaries

Blurred lines
Things people shouldn't say
Dark taboo and deep meanings
Slurred words and unhappy endings
Is it wrong to say no?
Or do you have to go along?

There was doubt in her eyes
Fuck this, she didn't want to do this
But she had to
If she could stop, she would, but she can't
This will never end
Pain, despair and doubt, anxiety, depression and hopelessness
And now it bores into her.

And

And never did she see something so beautiful
And ugly at the same time
And she covered them as best she could
But he saw through it anyway.

3 Lines, 3 Words

I place my hope inside a book, three lines, three words:
I'm
So
Sorry.

Unbroken Spell

It's wonderful she thought, the art on her skin.
It happens when she's all alone
It sounds like peace, a quiet unbroken spell
The beauty of her imperfect skin was wonderful she thought.

Speaking Bodies

My wrist spoke to my head
Disappointed with the wounds that bled
But my wrist smiled with glee
And said don't worry about me
My head tried to reason, just stop it said
Sometimes my wrist remembered the scars it had
Although that never stopped it from bleeding
My head screamed and yelled and started pleading.

My stomach said to my head it was okay I have those scars anyway.

Questionable

The blackbird has a secret
Will it tell,
Probably not.
You want to know so desperately
You beg and cry "Tell me, tell me your secret"
But the blackbird just nods its head and flies away.
You may never understand the secret
But the blackbird has already given you the answer.
So what was the question?

Get Back

And when the bird flies, all is lost to the wind
The beginning, a time when birds flew for pleasure, not to escape
And logic says that we must come down to earth at some point
But the heart brings pain that belongs in the mind
We meet that pain again
And the sun felt warm on their back and wings
Soon to overwhelm us once more.

Pain? Beauty?

Is it true that pain is beauty?
My skin is covered with proof
Long, snaking lines that smile up at me
Add more they say, eat less they say
Pain is beauty but I have suffered enough to be beautiful
A continuing cycle that never ends
Keep going they say, you need to do this
But is the outcome worth the price?

Resurrection

They are all back from the dead,
Those emotions and thoughts I thought I buried long ago
Now they rose, like a wave crashing against the insides of my mind,
Screaming and howling like the wind,
Ripping my insides out with a brutal force that took the air from my lungs and the logic in my head.
An internal conflict had arisen in my mind, one that only I could see
And I had no idea how to stop it.

Dwelling

Time to dwell in self-pity
Time to wait for time to pass
And hope that time will pass not so slowly
And hope that things will happen
Tide and time waits for no one
Tide and the clock that strikes six
Waits for dinner to be called
Waits to dwell in self-pity.

Caged

Well how did I get here
I don't remember much but I know I shouldn't be here,
Stuck, trapped, caged.
I should be free
I was going to be free but they stopped me.
Dragged me down by my wings,
Chained me to the earth and refused to let me fly,
Fly away to a place where I'd be sane.
But I'm not
I'm stuck because they denied me my freedom,
And deprived me of any emotions
Yes whitebird wants me safe but blackbird wants to fly…

Time and Time

Time to cry and feel those fears
Time and time goes too slow
And crying all those fears away
And hurting till it can hurt no more
Tide come to my waist
Tide come to my shoulders
Waits to slowly sink
Waits to slowly be swallowed away.

Breaking Down

Breaking down
Can't cope any more
Help me
Get me out of my own mind,

Can't cope anymore
Save me
Get me out of my own mind
I'm going crazy,

Save me
The voices won't go away
I'm going crazy
Leave me the fuck alone,

The voices won't go away
Help me
Leave me the fuck alone
Breaking down.

Outcast

Outcast
Pushed out and forgotten
Weird, strange, different
Forlorn, lost and alone,

Pushed out and forgotten
Like a piece of old furniture
Forlorn, lost and alone
But it's better that way,

Like a piece of old furniture
Used and abused
But it's better that way
All I am is a grievance,

Used and abused
Weird, strange, different
All I am is a grievance
Outcast.

Imperfectly Perfect

Your body's imperfectly perfect
Everybody wants what the other's working
Through the sheets of cloud, a mirror
A hazy image I hate.

Everybody wants what the other's working
But I'm still stuck with
A hazy image I hate
Drowning, lost in my own reflection.

But I'm still stuck with
All my imperfections
Drowning, lost in my own reflection
And the lies my mind tells me.

All my imperfections
Through the sheets of cloud, a mirror
And the lies my mind tells me
Your body's imperfectly perfect.

I am...

Pt.1

It lives in my soul, hidden deep within
I know exactly where to find it
It feels empty, expressionless, emotionless
I love it not, I fear it
It says things only I understand, things only I will do
I see death just out of reach, and although I try to grasp it I cannot
I am failure.

Pt.2

It lives on the surface of my skin
I know I cannot cover it up no matter how hard I try
It feels restless, always moving, always shaking
I love the control it has on my life
It says it lies but I don't know what to believe I see hazy images, none that I can grasp entirely
I am anxiety.

A Past Love

She looked so perfect standing there,
With a beautiful, flawless body
Would she ever love me
A broken vase, chunky fragments of glass shattered on the floor
A blanket of scars, tales from the past
Would she see me and hide fearful that it's contagious
Or would she embrace the mess and try to put the pieces back together?
Would she love the girl with the crisscrossed skin
Or would she find someone who could love her wholly, no issues
standing between
I'm a mess but I still hope that she would choose me.

My Body?

It's my body, I'll do what I like
But the moment you see my intentions you'll try to ruin my peace
The only peace I get is pain
You take this away yet it's my only way to cope and deal with the stress of being alive.
It's my body, I'll do what I like
Until you take over and control my life, again.

Sacred Scars

I dragged her through her darkest days
Pulled her up when she fell down,
Hid her scars when others looked,
Held her hands when she was scared,
But I was not enough
She still felt pain but found someone else to comfort her
Someone I could never be
I was never good enough for her no matter how hard I tried
And now I wonder if she was the one who tried to help me.

Fish

I am a fish in drowning waters and a bird in falling skies,
Wishing that my thoughts could fly.

Basket

In this basket is my soul,
Leaking through the cracks and edges,
Barely held together.

Salt Tears

Salt thrown behind her - superstitious about the bad
Salt behind her blinding the devil
Salt didn't work, he saw through it
Salt was useless.
Even in her tears,
Tears she cried
Tears that dried
Tears that she could not hide.

Lurking Bitterly

Sorrow is the shadow of death,
Like a crow picking at a corpse's flesh
Lingering when unwelcome
Lurking in the dark…waiting
You don't know when the brutality will hit,
But when it does, boy, you will know
Mournful melancholy
Bitter memories
Pain and aching in your limbs and heart,
There's no way you can escape this dark art.

Cigarettes

Some cry with tears; others with thoughts
And others bleed on paper
Raw emotions spilled across a page,
Each one more thick and bloody than before
Each one there to make you feel pain
Or maybe just emptiness
All your thoughts and feelings spread out on paper, leaving your body empty
Empty like a cigarette packet,
All the poison already used.
And too late to turn back.

Weather Forecast

It's raining knives again,
You would of thought my body would be used to it by now,
But each drop burns and serrates my skin
A hundred times over,
No umbrella for me
I should of checked the weather forecast in my mind before I set out
today,
It's raining knives again.

Tried and Failure Shelf

On the tried and failure shelf lay many things
Little draws and pockets of disappointment,
Jars of unaccounted guilt and bottles of emotional worry,
Caps and lids screwed on tight in hope they won't burst.
The shelf dipped and bent with the weight it held
Many, many failures and things tried long ago
It would be simple to just take the shelf down and discard its contents
But instead it's glue to the corners of my mind
Gathering dust and cobwebs only disturbed when another failure is plonked on top
Not very neat and barely organized,
What chaos it screamed to my orderly mind,
But file it away up there on the tried and failure shelf.

Imaginary Monsters

We are our own monsters
It's our imagination that lurks under the bed
Our feelings hidden at the back of the wardrobe
Waiting till it's dark to catch you off guard
But it's all in your head
Drawers of pain and guilt and disappointment
All opened with a single thought,
"Why can't I just be better?"
But no, you must suffer for all you have done.
The monsters drag out the pain until your mind is screaming
They won't stop until your tether is pulled taught, on the edge of breaking.
But the monsters won't snap it, won't let it end,
They keep it intact ready to torture you another day.

For Georgina

She had flowers for eyes
And little bees were drawn to them,
Blessing each flower as they passed.
They sung their way through the summer haze of her hair
It was the finest art,
To watch them weave between petals, sweet as the nectar they sought,
Each was the brilliant yellow of every sunny daydream with
reassuringly dark bands.
Aerodynamically bumble bees shouldn't be able to fly,
But they don't know this so they carry on flying anyway.
Ignorance is bliss but
Still a motherfucking killing machine.

Hunched is the Rook

Hunched is the blackbird, the rook, the raven
Upon a frost-bitten branch
All these blackbirds tell me secrets in my ear
Whisper, whisper like the wind in the trees

Hunched is the blackbird, the rook, the raven
Plunging down and down
I will not surrender but gravity takes me down
And I do the one thing I'm good at

Falling
Crashing
Lunging
Into the darkness

Where the blackbirds sit hunched
In the cold
And the wet
Frozen forever more.

Unconditional

There once was a girl
Who was pretty okay
She could write and read
Play sport and study

But then things started to fumble
Bubble, bubble, toil and trouble
And that girl was no longer okay
She was ill in the head
There were demons who taunted her
And angels who mocked

Unconditional pain
Anguish, suffering of the brain
"Help" she cried but
There was only darkness

Once she'd been in the dark
For so long
The girl was afraid of light.

Ramblings of Anger

So fucked up is society
With blurred lines
Slurred lines
Eating disorders
Mental disorders
Pain
Bane,

Worthless they say
You can't stay
In this world
You're not some pearl
The world is not your oyster
You will never prosper,

So fucked up is society
Be this, be that
Don't be such a twat
Wear this
It might not fit
But that doesn't matter
You'll never get better,

RAMBLINGS OF ANGER

Stuck in a box
Like an animal, a box
But I don't fit in
Bulging with sin
I overflow
I've got too much to show
But I keep it hidden
As would you in my position.

Slow down
Calm down
You're going to fast
But I'm running from the past
It keeps chasing me
Like I owe it some fee
Fuck off society
You're not so pretty
You sugar coat lies
That end lives
So fucked up.

Petition

One-by-one signatures were signed
Each a token of pride
Never did one feel so small
With a pen in one's hand and a cigarette to drawl
Coming and going
The river keeps flowing
But what if there was baggage
A loaded package
Dropped to the bottom
All wet and sodden
With somebody inside
Would it mater that they had signed
The petition
Repetition
The petition they signed
To end suicide.

What Makes A Monster

I drew a monster
A crazy, scary beast
With a white beard and so many teeth
A tail that forked
A mouth that talked
A hairy chest
And some clothes, no maybe less
Three cunning eyes
As perfect spies
And two little ears
That could hear your fears
Frightening he may be
But is he just a monster to me
Because what makes it a monster?

Rotten Pears

I'm staring at the ceiling
Wondering if there's a meaning
Of being there to help
When you're too far gone
And everything is coming undone.

I can't move my legs
Am I dead?
If only I was dead
Living fills me with such dread.

So many expectations
And celebrations
Of life
But listen to my strife.

I'm staring at the ceiling
Wondering what is the meaning
The meaning of dread
And do I really want to be dead?

Of course I do you silly fool

ROTTEN PEARS

What use are you
Silly brain
Sore and achy from strain.

I can't move my legs
And I've drunk the coffee dregs
Because life is unfair
And I get left with
Rotten pears.

Free?

This bird is not free
Maybe it was meant to be
But this bird could not see
It's destiny.

Was it to soar the skies
With a false disguise
Don't interrupt me with your fake demise
These little birds are so wise.

Listen to them talk
Such wisdom when they walk
All I can do is gawp
Their sense of humour is so warped.

Because this bird is trapped
This bird is tracked
And mapped
And entirely pissed off.

Stress

Make all your meals
And plan your week
Get into your feels
And talk about what you seek.

Make goals for the future
Forget about the past
One thing after another, it's a blur
Take it slow, but really fast.

Go to college and do really well
Manage your money
Put on a smile just to look swell
And pretend that you're funny.

Forget about your fear
And your anxiety
You'll be fine, hope is near
And they say just to drink tea.

Shower everyday
Then brush your teeth

TWO BIRDS AND A LOT MORE STONES

Remember those bills you have to pay
And get enough sleep.

Be happy, it's as simple as that
Put a smile on your face
Forget all that
Can't keep up with the pace.

Suicide is a Sin, They Say.

I can't close my eyes
Without thinking of death
Would it truly hurt
Or would I slip away
Peaceful and at ease
Finally put to rest
Or would my mind panic
My body unable
To wake up
My mind still spinning
And screaming
Gulping for air
But my lungs won't work
And I'm drowning
Suddenly in the sea
Freezing cold water
And I can't see
Falling
The air is sweet
But I can't seem to grasp any
Hitting the ground
Solid impact

TWO BIRDS AND A LOT MORE STONES

Nothing for a moment
Then pain
Would that be it
Or would I suffer eternally
For suicide is a sin
They say.

Drained of Colour

I'll go back to the colour of the abyss that lives inside my head,
Maybe that darkness is meant to be there,
Meant for me to stare into space,
Wondering what I've achieved in life,
If I've done enough,
Helped enough people,
Been kind enough.
But the colour says it all,
A burden,
Heavy on the universe somehow.
Not quite there,
Lost to the void,
And sucked into a deep, black hole.

Leave

Today I was granted leave,
To see and to walk free
For a bit at least
But not on my own, no
It's got to be with someone I know
A staff or family member
And I must remember
Not to run away really
Or do anything silly
So instead I'll just go
To the place I love
The stables.

Riding Once Again

It was completely normal,
Like a missing piece to a puzzle,
The moment she got on whitebird flew and blackbird chirped
She was free at last
At one with the beauty beneath her,
Her posture perfect,
Her pony willing
And nothing could stop her…

Firefly Stars

The stars are not afraid to appear like fireflies.
So maybe this is your sign to stand out,
To stand up for yourself,
To do something small but significant,
Or big and significant,
Up to you.
One star on its own is rarely seen,
But whole constellations light up the night sky.
So don't be afraid to do something tiny, big or small,
A step is a step towards recovery,
As every step is a star,
And every star is part of a beautiful constellation.

I Wish You Happiness

I wish you happiness. The kind where you can't stop laughing and your stomach aches; where you can't look at your friends without bursting into laughter all over again. I wish you the secret sly smiles you shoot your best friend across the room when your inside jokes come up in conversation. I wish you times where you go out shopping and try on pretty outfits that make you feel good about your body. I want you to be at peace with yourself and believe in yourself, your dreams and that healing is possible. I wish you happiness where you can talk endlessly about your interests to people who really want to listen to you because you sound so passionate about them. I wish you happiness where you are on your phone for hours sending silly memes or telling jokes to the people you care about just to cheer them up.

Printed in Dunstable, United Kingdom